Steps to *FREEDOM IN CHRIST*

Other Neil Anderson titles published by Monarch Books:

The Bondage Breaker (Study Guide Edition)
Daily In Christ (New Edition)
Freedom from Fear
Higher Ground
Living Free
Righteous Pursuit
Set Free (Omnibus Edition)
Victory Over the Darkness (Study Guide Edition)

Available from Christian bookshops or, if in difficulty, contact Monarch Books, Concorde House, Grenville Place, Mill Hill, London NW7 3SA.

Steps to *FREEDOM IN CHRIST*

Dr NEIL T. ANDERSON

MONARCH
BOOKS

First published for the UK in 2000 by Monarch Books.

ISBN 1 85424 489 2

Unless otherwise stated, Scripture quotations are
taken from *New American Standard Bible*,
© 1960, 1962, 1963, 1971, 1972, 1973, 1975, 1977 by
The Lockman Foundation. Used by permission.
All rights reserved.

British Library Cataloguing Data
A catalogue record for this book is available
from the British Library.

Designed and produced for the publisher by
Gazelle Creative Productions Ltd,
Concorde House, Grenville Place, Mill Hill, London NW7 3SA.

Contents

Foreword

By Steve Goss, Director, Freedom In Christ Ministries (UK)

If you seem to be going round in circles as a Christian, if you sense that you are simply not growing as you should be, if you struggle in your thought life, or if you are stuck in a cycle of sin-confess-sin-confess that you can't seem to break, then *Steps To Freedom In Christ* can help.

Over the last couple of years I have been amazed at how Christians in the UK have used *Steps To Freedom In Christ* to claim lasting freedom from past experiences, bad habits and many other negative influences. 'Hard cases' have been set free to experience God's love and purpose in a new way. 'Ordinary' Christians have been able to grasp, perhaps for the first time, just how much God loves them and then move on to levels of maturity that had seemed out of reach.

That's why I am delighted – and excited – that there is now a version especially for UK Christians. I know that it will prove significant to the Church in this country.

But this is no 'magic formula', no zany self-help product – it's pure biblical truth in a very helpful package. After all, it's not the Steps that set you free – it's Jesus Christ.

To get the full benefit you'll need to be prepared to do some work. If you are serious about claiming the freedom that Christ has already won for you, and want to avoid falling back into unproductive ways of thinking, it's essential that you take time to understand what the Bible says about who you are in Christ. The best way I know to do this is to read Neil Anderson's main books, *Victory Over the Darkness* and *The Bondage Breaker*. Read them before you go through the steps and again afterwards.

Then why not help your fellow Christians to claim their freedom too! One of the best things about *Steps To Freedom In Christ* is that it can be used as the basis of a highly effective ministry in the local church. The concepts are designed for lay people rather than specialists and are completely transferable. Ministries based on them have revolutionised churches around the world – why not yours? (For more details of the many resources available to help churches establish freedom ministries, see *How To Establish A Freedom Ministry in Your Church*.)

If the enemy is telling you this won't work for you, don't listen – when Jesus said that He would set you free, He meant it!

Introduction

It is my deep conviction that the finished work of Jesus Christ and the presence of God in our lives are the only means by which we can resolve our personal and spiritual conflicts. Christ in us is our only hope (see Colossians 1:27), and He alone can meet our deepest needs in life: acceptance, identity, security and significance. The discipleship counselling process upon which these steps are based should not be understood as just another counselling technique that we learn. It is an encounter with God. He is the Wonderful Counsellor. He is the One who grants repentance that leads to a knowledge of the truth which sets us free (2 Timothy 2:25, 26).

The Steps to Freedom in Christ do not set you free. *Who* sets you free is Christ, and *what* sets you free is your response to Him in repentance and faith. These Steps are just a tool to help you submit to God and resist the devil (James 4:7). Then you can start living a fruitful life by abiding in Christ and becoming the person He created you to be. Many Christians will be able to work through these steps on their own and discover the wonderful freedom that Christ purchased for them on the cross. Then they will experience the peace of God which transcends all understanding, and it will guard their hearts and their minds (Philippians 4:7).

Before you begin

The chances of that happening and the possibility of maintaining that freedom will be greatly enhanced if you read *Victory Over the Darkness* and *The Bondage Breaker* first. Many Christians in the western world need to understand the reality of the spiritual world and our relationship to it. Some can't read these books or even the Bible with comprehension because of the battle that is going on for their minds. They will need the assistance of others who have been trained. The theology and practical process of discipleship counselling is given in my book, *Helping Others Find Freedom in Christ*, and the accompanying *Training Manual and Study Guide* and Video Training Programme. The book attempts to integrate biblically the reality of the spiritual and the natural world so we can have a whole answer for a whole person. In doing so, we cannot polarise into psychotherapeutic ministries that ignore the reality of the spiritual world or attempt some kind of deliverance ministry that ignores developmental issues and human responsibility.

You may need help

Ideally, it would be best if everyone had a trusted friend, minister or counsellor who would help them go through this process because it is just applying the wisdom of James 5:16: 'Therefore confess your sins to each other and pray for each other so that you may be healed. The prayer of a righteous man is powerful and effective.' Another person can prayerfully support you by providing objective counsel – I have had the privilege of helping many Christian leaders who could not go through the process on their own. Many Christian groups all over the world are using this approach in many languages with incredible results because the Lord desires for all to come to repentance (2 Peter 3:9), and to know the truth that sets us free in Christ (John 8:32).

Appropriating and maintaining freedom

Christ has set us free through His victory over sin and death on the cross. However, appropriating our freedom in Christ through repentance and faith and maintaining our life of freedom in Christ are two different issues. It was for freedom that Christ set us free, but we have been warned not to return to a yoke of slavery, which in this context is legalism (Galatians 5:1), or to turn our freedom into an opportunity for the flesh (Galatians 5:13). Establishing people free in Christ makes it possible for them to walk by faith according to what God says is true, to live by the power of the Holy Spirit and not to carry out the desires of the flesh (Galatians 5:16). The true Christian life avoids both legalism and licence.

If you are not experiencing freedom, it may be because you have not stood firm in the faith or actively taken your place in Christ. It is every Christian's responsibility to do whatever is necessary to maintain a right relationship with God and mankind. Your eternal destiny is not at stake. God will never leave you or forsake you (Hebrews 13:5), but your daily victory is at stake if you fail to claim and maintain your position in Christ.

Your position in Christ

You are not a helpless victim caught between two nearly equal but opposite heavenly superpowers. Satan is a deceiver. Only God is all-powerful, always present and all-knowing. Sometimes the reality of sin and the presence of evil may seem more real than the presence of God, but that's part of Satan's deception. Satan is a defeated foe and we are in Christ. A true knowledge of God and knowing our identity and position in Christ are the greatest determinants of our mental health. A false concept of God, a distorted understanding of who we are as children of God, and making Satan out to be as powerful and present as God are the greatest contributors to mental illness.

Many of our illnesses are psychosomatic. When these issues are resolved in Christ, our physical bodies will function better and we will experience greater health. Other problems are clearly physical and we need the services of the medical profession. Please consult your GP for medical advice and the prescribing of medication. We are both spiritual and physical beings who need the services of both the Church and the medical profession.

Winning the battle for your mind

The battle is for our minds, the control centres of all that we think and do. The opposing thoughts you may experience as you go through these steps can control you only if you believe them. If you are working through these steps alone, don't be deceived by any lying, intimidating thoughts in your mind. If a trusted minister or counsellor is helping you find freedom in Christ, he or she must have your co-operation. You must share any thoughts you are having that oppose what you are attempting to do. As soon as you expose the lie, the power of Satan is broken. The only way that you can lose control in this process is if you pay attention to a deceiving spirit and believe a lie.

You must choose

The following procedure is a means of resolving personal and spiritual conflicts which have kept you from experiencing the freedom and victory Christ purchased for you on the cross. Your freedom will be the result of what *you* choose to believe, confess, forgive, renounce and forsake. No one can do that for you. The battle for your mind can only be won as you personally choose truth. As you go through this process, understand that Satan is under no obligation to obey your thoughts. Only God has complete knowledge of your mind because He is all-knowing. So we can submit to God inwardly, but we need to resist the devil by reading aloud each prayer and by verbally renouncing, forgiving, confessing, etc.

This process of re-establishing our freedom in Christ is nothing more than a fierce moral inventory and a rock-solid commitment to truth. It is the first step in the continuing process of discipleship. There is no such thing as instant maturity. It will take you the rest of your life to renew your mind and conform to the image of God. If your problems stem from a source other than those covered in these steps, you may need to seek professional help.

May the Lord grace you with His presence as you seek His face and help others experience the joy of their salvation.

Prayer

Dear Heavenly Father,
We acknowledge Your presence in this room and in our lives. You are the only all-knowing, all-powerful, and ever-present God. We are dependent upon You, for apart from You we can do nothing. We stand in the truth that all authority in heaven and on earth has been given to the resurrected Christ, and because we are in Christ, we share that authority in order to make disciples and set captives free. We ask You to fill us with Your Holy Spirit and lead us into all truth. We pray for Your complete protection and ask for Your guidance. In Jesus' name, amen.

Declaration

In the name and authority of the Lord Jesus Christ, we command Satan and all evil spirits to release (name) in order that (name) can be free to know and choose to do the will of God. As children of God seated with Christ in the heavenlies, we agree that every enemy of the Lord Jesus Christ be bound to silence. We say to Satan and all your evil workers that you cannot inflict any pain or in any way prevent God's will from being accomplished in (name's) life.

Preparation

Before going through the Steps to Freedom, review the events of your life to discern specific areas that might need to be addressed.

Family History

___ Religious history of parents and grandparents

___ Home life from childhood through to secondary school

___ History of physical or emotional illness in the family

___ Adoption, foster care, guardians

Personal History

___ Eating habits (bulimia, bingeing and purging, anorexia, compulsive eating)

___ Addictions (drugs, alcohol)

___ Prescription medications (what for?)

___ Sleeping patterns and nightmares

___ Rape or any other sexual, physical, or emotional abuse

___ Thought life (obsessive, blasphemous, condemning, distracting thoughts, poor concentration, fantasy)

___ Mental interference during church, prayer or Bible study

___ Emotional life (anger, anxiety, depression, bitterness, fears)

___ Spiritual journey (salvation: when, how and assurance)

Now you are ready to begin. The following are seven specific steps to go through in order to experience freedom from your past. You will address the areas where Satan most commonly takes advantage of us where strongholds have been built.

If your problems stem from a source other than those covered in these steps, you have nothing to lose by going through them. If you are sincere, the only thing that can happen is that you will get right with God!

Step 1
Counterfeit vs. Real

The first Step to Freedom in Christ is to renounce your previous or current involvement with satanically inspired occult practices and false religions. You need to renounce any activity or group that denies Jesus Christ, offers guidance through any source other than the absolute authority of the written Word of God, or requires secret initiations, ceremonies or covenants.

In order to help you assess your spiritual experiences, begin this step by asking God to reveal false guidance and counterfeit religious experiences.

Dear Heavenly Father,
I ask You to guard my heart and my mind and reveal to me any and all involvement I have had either knowingly or unknowingly with cultic or occult practices, false religions or false teachers. In Jesus' name, I pray. Amen.

Using the Non-Christian Spiritual Experience Inventory, carefully mark off anything in which you have been involved. This list is not exhaustive, but it will guide you in identifying non-Christian experiences. Add any additional involvement you have had. Even if you innocently participated in something or observed it, you should write it on your list to renounce, just in case you unknowingly gave Satan a foothold.

Non-Christian Spiritual Experience Inventory

(Please tick those that apply)

- ❏ Astral projection
- ❏ Ouija board
- ❏ Table or body lifting
- ❏ Dungeons and Dragons
- ❏ Speaking in trance
- ❏ Automatic writing
- ❏ Telepathy
- ❏ Using spells or curses
- ❏ Séance
- ❏ Materialisation
- ❏ Clairvoyance
- ❏ Spirit guides
- ❏ Fortune-telling
- ❏ Tarot cards
- ❏ Palm reading
- ❏ Astrology/ horoscopes
- ❏ Rod/pendulum (dowsing)
- ❏ Self-hypnosis
- ❏ Mental manipulations or attempts to swap minds
- ❏ Black and white magic
- ❏ New Age medicine

- ❏ Blood pacts or self-mutilation
- ❏ Fetishism (objects of worship, crystals, good luck charms)
- ❏ Incubi and succubi (sexual spirits)
- ❏ Occult or violent video or computer games
- ❏ Horror films, books, magazines
- ❏ Superstition (touching wood, salt over shoulder, Friday 13th)
- ❏ Other

  _____

- ❏ Buddhism
- ❏ Hare Krishna
- ❏ Bahaism
- ❏ Science of the Mind
- ❏ Transcendental Meditation
- ❏ Hinduism
- ❏ Yoga
- ❏ Roy Masters
- ❏ Silva Mind Control

- ❏ Father Divine
- ❏ Theosophical Society
- ❏ Islam
- ❏ Black Muslim
- ❏ Religion of martial arts
- ❏ Rosicrucianism
- ❏ Other

  _____

- ❏ Christian Science
- ❏ Unity
- ❏ The Way International
- ❏ Unification Church
- ❏ Mormonism
- ❏ Church of the Living Word
- ❏ Jehovah's Witnesses
- ❏ Children of God (Love)
- ❏ Masons or other secret society
- ❏ New Age
- ❏ The Forum (EST)
- ❏ Spirit Worship
- ❏ Other

  _____

1. Have you ever been hypnotised, attended a New Age or parapsychology seminar, consulted a medium, spiritist or channeller? Explain.

_____

_____

2. Do you have or have you ever had an imaginary friend or spirit guide offering you guidance or companionship? Explain.

_____

_____

3. Have you ever heard voices in your mind or had repeating and nagging thoughts condemning you or that were foreign to what you believe or feel, as if there were a dialogue going on in your head? Explain.

_____

_____

4. What other spiritual experiences have you had that would be considered out of the ordinary?

_____

_____

5. Have you ever made a vow, covenant or pact with any individual or group other than God?

_____

_____

6. Have you been involved in satanic ritual or satanic worship in any form? Explain.

_____

When you are confident that your list is complete, confess and renounce each involvement whether active or passive by praying aloud the following prayer, repeating it separately for each item on your list:

Lord Jesus,
I confess that I have participated in _____
(activity), and I renounce_____ (activity)
and any effect it has had in my life. Thank You that in
Christ I am forgiven.

If there has been any involvement in satanic ritual or heavy occult activity, you need to state aloud the following renunciations that apply. Read across the page, renouncing the first item in the column of the Kingdom of Darkness and then affirming the first truth in the column of the Kingdom of Light. Continue down opposite the page in this manner.

All satanic rituals, covenants and assignments must be specifically renounced as the Lord allows you to recall them. Some who have been subjected to satanic ritual abuse may have developed multiple personalities in order to survive. Nevertheless, continue through the Steps to Freedom in order to resolve all that you consciously can. It is important that you resolve the demonic strongholds first. Every personality must resolve his/her issues and agree to come together in Christ. You may need someone who understands spiritual conflict to help maintain control and not be deceived into false memories. Only Jesus can bind up the broken-hearted, set captives free and make us whole.

Kingdom of Darkness	Kingdom of Light
I renounce ever signing my name over to Satan or having had my name signed over to Satan.	I announce that my name is now written in the Lamb's Book of Life.
I renounce any ceremony where I might have been wed to Satan.	I announce that I am the bride of Christ.
I renounce any and all covenants that I made with Satan.	I announce that I am a partaker of the New Covenant with Christ.
I renounce all satanic assignments for my life, including duties, marriage and children.	I announce and commit myself to know and do only the will of God and accept only His guidance.
I renounce all spirit guides assigned to me.	I announce and accept only the leading of the Holy Spirit.
I renounce ever giving of my blood in the service of Satan.	I trust only in the shed blood of my Lord Jesus Christ.
I renounce ever eating of flesh or drinking of blood for satanic worship.	By faith I take Holy Communion which represents the body and the blood of the Lord Jesus.
I renounce any and all guardians and satanist parents who were assigned to me.	I announce that God is my Father and the Holy Spirit is my Guardian by which I am sealed.
I renounce any baptism in blood or urine whereby I am identified with Satan.	I announce that I have been baptised into Christ Jesus and my identity is now in Christ.
I renounce any and all sacrifices that were made on my behalf by which Satan may claim ownership of me.	I announce that only the sacrifice of Christ has any hold on me. I belong to Him. I have been purchased by the blood of the Lamb.

Step 2
Deception vs. Truth

Truth is the revelation of God's Word, but we need to acknowledge the truth in our inner self (Psalm 51:6). When David lived a lie, he suffered greatly. When he finally found freedom by acknowledging the truth, he wrote: 'Blessed is the man ... in whose spirit is no deceit' (Psalm 32:2). We are to lay aside falsehood and speak the truth in love (Ephesians 4:15, 25). A mentally healthy person is one who is in touch with reality and relatively free of anxiety. Both qualities should characterise the Christian who renounces deception and embraces the truth.

Begin this critical step by saying aloud the following prayer. Don't let the enemy accuse you with thoughts such as: *This isn't going to work* or *I wish I could believe this, but I can't* or any other lies in opposition to what you are proclaiming. Even if you have difficulty doing so, you need to pray the prayer and read the Doctrinal Affirmation.

Dear Heavenly Father,
I know that You desire truth in the inner self and that facing this truth is the way of liberation (John 8:32). I acknowledge that I have been deceived by the father of lies (John 8:44) and that I have deceived myself (1 John 1:8). I pray in the name of the Lord Jesus Christ

that You, Heavenly Father, will rebuke all deceiving spirits by virtue of the shed blood and resurrection of the Lord Jesus Christ. By faith I received You into my life and I am now seated with Christ in the heavenlies (Ephesians 2:6). I acknowledge that I have the responsibility and authority to resist the devil, and when I do, he will flee from me. I now ask the Holy Spirit to guide me into all truth (John 16:13). I ask You to 'Search me, O God, and know my heart; test me and know my anxious thoughts. See if there is any offensive way in me, and lead me in the way everlasting' (Psalm 139:23, 24). In Jesus' name, I pray. Amen.

You may want to pause at this point to consider some of Satan's deceptive schemes. In addition to false teachers, false prophets and deceiving spirits, you can be deceived by yourself. Now that you are alive in Christ and forgiven, you never have to live a lie or defend yourself. Christ is your defence. How have you deceived or attempted to defend yourself instead of trusting in Christ? Please tick any of the following that apply to you:

Self-Deception

❏ Hearing God's Word but not doing it (James 1:22; 4:17)

❏ Saying you have no sin (1 John 1:8)

❏ Thinking you are something when you aren't (Galatians 6:3)

❏ Thinking you are wise in your own eyes (1 Corinthians 3:18, 19)

❏ Thinking you will not reap what you sow (Galatians 6:7)

- ❑ Thinking the unrighteous will inherit the kingdom (1 Corinthians 6:9)
- ❑ Thinking you can associate with bad company and not be corrupted (1 Corinthians 15:33)

Self-Defence

- ❑ Denial (conscious or subconscious refusal to face the truth)
- ❑ Fantasy (escaping from the real world)
- ❑ Emotional insulation (withdrawing to avoid rejection)
- ❑ Regression (reverting back to a less threatening time)
- ❑ Displacement (taking out frustrations on others)
- ❑ Projection (blaming others)
- ❑ Rationalisation (making excuses for poor behaviour)
- ❑ Lying

For each of those things that you have ticked, pray aloud:

Lord Jesus,
I agree that I have been deceiving myself in the area of
_____ (area).
Thank You for forgiving me. I commit myself to know and follow Your truth. Amen.

Choosing the truth may be difficult if you have been living a lie (being deceived) for many years. You may need to seek professional help to weed out the defence mechanisms you have depended upon to survive. The Christian needs only one defence – Jesus. Knowing that you are forgiven and accepted as God's child is what sets you free to face reality and declare your dependence on Him.

Faith is the biblical response to the truth and believing the truth is a choice. When someone says, 'I want to believe God, but I just can't,' they are being deceived. Of course you can believe God. Faith is something you decide to do, not something you feel like doing. Believing the truth doesn't make it true. It's true; therefore we believe it. The New Age movement is distorting the truth by saying we create reality through what we believe. We can't create reality with our minds; we face reality. It is what or who you believe in that counts. Everybody believes in something, and everybody walks by faith according to what he or she believes. But if what you believe isn't true, then how you live (walk by faith) won't be right.

Historically, the Church has found great value in publicly declaring its beliefs. The Apostles' Creed and the Nicene Creed have been recited for centuries. Read aloud the following affirmation of faith, and do so again as often as necessary to renew your mind. Experiencing difficulty reading the affirmation may indicate where you are being deceived and under attack. Boldly affirm your commitment to biblical truth.

Doctrinal Affirmation

I recognise that there is only one true and living God (Exodus 20:2, 3) who exists as the Father, Son and Holy Spirit and that He is worthy of all honour, praise and glory as the Creator, Sustainer and Beginning and End of all things (Revelation 4:11; 5:9, 10; 22:13; Isaiah 43:1, 7, 21).

I recognise Jesus Christ as the Messiah, the Word who became flesh and dwelt among us (John 1:1, 14). I believe that He came to destroy the works of Satan (1 John 3:8), that He disarmed the rulers and authorities and made a public display of them, having triumphed over them (Colossians 2:15).

I believe that God has proved His love for me because when I was still a sinner, Christ died for me (Romans 5:8). I believe that He delivered me from the domain of darkness, and transferred me to His kingdom, and in Him I have redemption – the forgiveness of sins (Colossians 1:13, 14).

I believe that I am now a child of God (1 John 3:1–3) and I am seated with Christ in the heavenlies (Ephesians 2:6). I believe that I was saved by the grace of God through faith, that it was a gift, and not the result of any works on my part (Ephesians 2:8, 9).

I choose to be strong in the Lord and in the strength of His might (Ephesians 6:10). I put no confidence in the flesh (Philippians 3:3), for the weapons of warfare are not of the flesh (2 Corinthians 10:4). I put on the whole armour of God (Ephesians 6:10–20), and I resolve to stand firm in my faith and resist the evil one.

I believe that apart from Christ I can do nothing (John 15:5), so I declare myself dependent on Him. I choose to abide in Christ in order to bear much fruit and glorify the Lord (John 15:8). I announce to Satan that Jesus is my Lord (1 Corinthians 12:3), and I reject any counterfeit gifts or works of Satan in my life.

I believe that the truth will set me free (John 8:32) and that walking in the light is the only path of fellowship

(1 John 1:7). Therefore, I stand against Satan's deception by taking every thought captive in obedience to Christ (2 Corinthians 10:5). I declare that the Bible is the only authoritative standard (2 Timothy 3:15, 16). I choose to speak the truth in love (Ephesians 4:15).

I choose to present my body as an instrument of righteousness, a living and holy sacrifice, and I renew my mind by the living Word of God in order that I may prove that the will of God is good, acceptable and perfect (Romans 6:13; 12:1, 2). I put off the old self with its evil practices and put on the new self (Colossians 3:9, 10), and I declare myself to be a new creation in Christ (2 Corinthians 5:17).

I trust my heavenly Father to fill me with His Holy Spirit (Ephesians 5:18), to lead me into all truth (John 16:13), and to empower my life that I may live above sin and not carry out the desires of the flesh (Galatians 5:16). I crucify the flesh (Galatians 5:24) and choose to walk by the Spirit.

I renounce all selfish goals and choose the ultimate goal of love (1 Timothy 1:5). I choose to obey the two greatest commandments: to love the Lord my God with all my heart, soul and mind, and to love my neighbour as myself (Matthew 22:37–39).

I believe that Jesus has all authority in heaven and on earth (Matthew 28:18) and He is the Head over all rule and authority (Colossians 2:10). I believe that Satan and his demons are subject to me in Christ since I am a member of Christ's Body (Ephesians 1:19–23). Therefore, I obey the command to submit to God and resist the devil (James 4:7), and I command Satan in the name of Christ to leave my presence.

Step 3
Bitterness vs. Forgiveness

We need to forgive others in order to be free from our past and to prevent Satan from taking advantage of us (2 Corinthians 2:10, 11). We are to be merciful just as our heavenly Father is merciful (Luke 6:36). We are to forgive as we have been forgiven (Ephesians 4:31, 32). Ask God to bring to mind the names of those people you need to forgive by praying the following prayer aloud.

Dear Heavenly Father,
I thank You for the riches of Your kindness,
forbearance and patience, knowing that Your kindness
has led me to repentance (Romans 2:4). I confess that I
have not extended that same patience and kindness
toward others who have offended me, but instead I
have harboured bitterness and resentment. I pray that
during this time of self-examination You would bring
to my mind those people whom I need to forgive in
order that I may do so (Matthew 18:35). I ask this in
the precious name of Jesus. Amen.

As names come to mind, list them on the following page or on a separate sheet of paper. At the end of your list, write 'myself'. Forgiving yourself is accepting God's cleansing and forgiveness. Also, write 'thoughts against God'. Thoughts raised up against the knowledge of God will usually result in angry feelings toward Him. Technically, we don't forgive God because He cannot commit any sin of commission or omission. But we do need to renounce false expectations and thoughts about God and agree to release any anger we have toward Him.

Before you pray to forgive these people, stop and consider what forgiveness is, what it is not, what decision you will be making and what the consequences will be. In the following explanation, the main points are in bold print:

Forgiveness is not forgetting. People who try to forget find they cannot. God says He will remember our sins no more (Hebrews 10:17). But God, being omniscient, cannot forget. 'Remember our sins no more' means that God will never use the past against us (Psalm 103:12). Forgetting may be the result of forgiveness, but it is never the means of forgiveness. When we bring up the past against others, we are saying we haven't forgiven them.

Forgiveness is a choice, a crisis of the will. Since God requires us to forgive, it is something we can do. However, forgiveness is difficult for us because it pulls against our concept of justice. We want revenge for offences suffered. However, we are told never to take our own revenge (Romans 12:19). You say, 'Why should I let them off the hook?' That is precisely the problem. You are still hooked to them, still bound by your past. **You can let them off your hook, but they are never off God's.** He will deal with them fairly – something we cannot do.

You say, 'You don't understand how much this person hurt me!' But don't you see, they are still hurting you! How do you stop the pain? **You don't forgive someone for their sake; you do it for your own sake so you can be free.** Your need to forgive isn't an issue between you and the offender; it's between you and God.

Forgiveness is agreeing to live with the consequences of another person's sin. Forgiveness is costly. You pay the price of the evil you forgive. You're going to live with those consequences whether you want to or not; your only choice is whether you will do so in the bitterness of unforgiveness or the freedom of forgiveness. Jesus took the consequences of your sin upon Himself. We need to accept the temporary consequences of what was done to us. No one really forgives without bearing the consequences of the other person's sin. God the Father 'made him who had no sin to be sin for us, so that in him we might become the righteousness of God' (2 Corinthians 5:21). Where is the justice? It's the cross that makes forgiveness legally and morally right: 'The death he died, he died to sin once for all' (Romans 6:10).

Decide that you will bear the burdens of their offences by not using that information against them in the future. This doesn't mean that you tolerate sin. You must set up scriptural boundaries to prevent future abuse. Some may be required to testify for the sake of justice but not for the purpose of seeking revenge from a bitter heart.

How do you forgive from your heart? You acknowledge the hurt and the hate. If your forgiveness doesn't visit the emotional core of your life, it will be incomplete. Many feel the pain of interpersonal offences, but they won't or don't know how to acknowledge it. Let God bring the pain to the surface so He can deal with it. This is where the healing takes place.

Don't wait to forgive until you feel like forgiving; you will never get there. Feelings take time to heal after the choice to forgive is made and Satan has lost his place (Ephesians 4:26, 27). **Freedom is what will be gained, not a feeling.**

As you pray, God may bring to mind offending people and experiences you have totally forgotten. Let Him do it even if it is painful. Remember, you are doing this for your sake. God wants you to be free. Don't rationalise or explain the offender's behaviour. Forgiveness is dealing with your pain and leaving the other person to God. Positive feelings will follow in time; freeing you from the past is the critical issue right now.

Don't say, 'Lord, please help me to forgive,' because He is already helping you. Don't say, 'Lord, I want to forgive,' because you are bypassing the hard-core choice to forgive, which is your responsibility. Focus on each individual until you are sure you have dealt with all the remembered pain – what they did, how they hurt you, how they made you feel: rejected, unloved, unworthy, dirty, etc.

You are now ready to forgive the people on your list so you can be free in Christ, with those people no longer having any control over you. For each person on your list, pray aloud:

Lord,
I forgive_____ (person) for _____
_____
(verbally share every hurt and pain the Lord brings to your mind and how it made you feel).

After you have forgiven every person for every painful memory, then finish this step by praying:

Lord,
I release all these people to You, and I release my right to seek revenge. I choose not to hold on to my bitterness and anger, and I ask You to heal my damaged emotions. In Jesus' name, I pray. Amen.

Many people find Appendix 1 useful at this stage. It helps us affirm the wonderful truth of our Father God's intimate love for us, something that is especially important for those brought up with a distant concept of God or whose earthly fathers have not been all they could have been.

Step 4
Rebellion vs. Submission

We live in rebellious times. Many believe it is their right to sit in judgement of those in authority over them. Rebelling against God and His authority gives Satan an opportunity to attack. As our commanding General, the Lord tells us to get into ranks and follow Him; He will not lead into temptation, but will deliver us from evil (Matthew 6:13).

We have two biblical responsibilities regarding authority figures: pray for them and submit to them. The only time God permits us to disobey earthly leaders is when they require us to do something morally wrong before God or attempt to rule outside the realm of their authority. Pray the following prayer:

Dear Heavenly Father,
You have said that rebellion is like the sin of witchcraft and being self-willed is like serving false gods (1 Samuel 15:23). I know that in action and attitude I have sinned against You with a rebellious heart. Thank You for forgiving my rebellion, and I pray that by the shed blood of the Lord Jesus Christ all ground gained by evil spirits because of my rebelliousness will be cancelled. I pray that You will shed light on all my ways that I may know the full extent of my rebelliousness. I choose to adopt a submissive spirit and a servant's heart. In the name of Christ Jesus, my Lord, Amen.

Being under authority is an act of faith. You are trusting God to work through His established lines of authority. There are times when employers, parents and husbands violate the laws of civil government, which are ordained by God to protect innocent people against abuse. In these cases, you need to appeal to the state for your protection. In many countries, the law requires such abuse to be reported.

In difficult cases, such as continuing abuse at home, further counselling help may be needed. And, in some cases, when earthly authorities have abused their position and are requiring disobedience to God or a compromise in your commitment to Him, you need to obey God, not man.

We are all told to submit to one another as equals in Christ (Ephesians 5:21). However, there are specific lines of authority in Scripture for the purpose of accomplishing common goals:

❏ Civil government (Romans 13:1–7; 1 Timothy 2:1–4; 1 Peter 2:13–17)

❏ Parents (Ephesians 6:1–3)

❏ Husband (1 Peter 3:1–4) or wife (Ephesians 5:21; 1 Peter 3:7)

❏ Employers (1 Peter 2:18–23)

❏ Church leaders (Hebrews 13:17)

❏ God (Daniel 9:5, 9)

❏ Examine each area and confess those times you have not been submissive by praying:

Lord,
I agree I have been rebellious towards _____
(person/institution). I choose to be submissive and obedient to Your Word. In Jesus' name, Amen.

Step 5
Pride vs. Humility

Pride is a killer. Pride says, 'I can do it! I can get myself out of this mess without God's or anyone else's help.' Oh no, we can't! We absolutely need God, and we desperately need each other. Paul wrote: 'For it is ... we who worship by the Spirit of God, who glory in Christ Jesus, and who put no confidence in the flesh' (Philippians 3:3). Humility is confidence properly placed. We are to be 'strong in the Lord and in his mighty power' (Ephesians 6:10). James 4:6–10 and 1 Peter 5:1–10 reveal that spiritual conflict follows pride. Use the following prayer to express your commitment to live humbly before God:

Dear Heavenly Father,
You have said that pride goes before destruction and an arrogant spirit before stumbling (Proverbs 16:18). I confess that I have lived independently and have not denied myself, picked up my cross daily and followed You (Matthew 16:24). In so doing, I have given ground to the enemy in my life. I have believed that I could be successful and live victoriously by my own strength and resources. I now confess that I have sinned against You by placing my will before Yours and by centring my life around myself instead of You. I now renounce the self-life and by so doing cancel all the ground that has been gained in my members by the enemies of the Lord Jesus Christ. I pray that You will guide me so that I will do nothing from selfishness or empty conceit, but

with humility of mind I will regard others as more important than myself (Philippians 2:3). Enable me through love to serve others and in honour prefer others (Romans 12:10). I ask this in the name of Christ Jesus, my Lord. Amen.

Having made that commitment, now allow God to show you any specific area of your life where you have been prideful, such as:

❑ Having a stronger desire to do my will than God's will

❑ Being more dependent on my strengths and resources than God's

❑ Too often believing that my ideas and opinions are better than others'

❑ Being more concerned about controlling others than developing self-control

❑ Sometimes considering myself more important than others

❑ Having a tendency to think that I have no needs

❑ Finding it difficult to admit that I was wrong

❑ Having a tendency to be more of a people-pleaser than a God-pleaser

❑ Being overly concerned about getting the credit I deserve

❑ Being driven to obtain the recognition that comes from degrees, titles and positions

❑ Often thinking I am more humble than others

❑ These other ways: _____

For each of these that has been true in your life, pray aloud:

_____

Lord,
I agree I have been prideful by _____
(act/tendency). I choose to humble myself and place all my confidence in You. Amen.

Step 6
Bondage vs. Freedom

The next Step to Freedom deals with the sins that have become habits in your life. People who have been caught in the trap of sin-confess-sin-confess may need to follow the instructions of James 5:16, 'Confess your sins to each other and pray for each other so that you may be healed. The prayer of a righteous man is powerful and effective.' Seek out a stronger Christian who will lift you up in prayer and hold you accountable in your areas of weakness. Others may only need the assurance of 1 John 1:9: 'If we confess our sins, He is faithful and just and will forgive us our sins and purify us from all unrighteousness.'

Confession is not saying 'I'm sorry;' it's saying 'I did it.' Whether you need the help of others or just the accountability to God, pray the following prayer:

Dear Heavenly Father,
You have told us to put on the Lord Jesus Christ and not to think about how to gratify our sinful desires (Romans 13:14). I agree that I have given in to fleshly desires which wage war against my soul (1 Peter 2:11). I thank You that in Christ my sins are forgiven, but I have broken Your holy law and given the enemy an opportunity to wage war in my physical body (Romans 6:12, 13; Ephesians 4:27; James 4:1; 1 Peter 5:8). I

come before Your presence to admit these sins and to seek Your cleansing (1 John 1:9), that I may be freed from the bondage of sin. I now ask You to reveal to my mind the ways that I have broken Your moral law and grieved the Holy Spirit. In Jesus' precious name, I pray. Amen.

There are many habitual sins that might control us. Many of the following issues are from Galatians 5:19–21. Look through the following list and ask the Holy Spirit to reveal to your mind which ones from the past or present you have been guilty of. He may bring to mind others that are not here. For each one God reveals, pray the following prayer of confession from the heart.

Note: Sexual sins, eating disorders, substance abuse, abortion, suicidal tendencies, perfectionism and fear will be dealt with later in this Step.

❑ Stealing

❑ Lying

❑ Fighting

❑ Jealousy

❑ Envying

❑ Outbursts of anger

❑ Quarrelling/arguing

❑ Complaining

❑ Criticising

❑ Lusting

❑ Cheating

❑ Gossiping

❑ Controlling

❑ Gambling

❑ Procrastinating – putting things off

❑ Swearing

❑ Greediness

❑ Laziness

❑ Divisiveness

❑ Other _____

Dear Heavenly Father,
I thank You that my sins are forgiven in Christ, but I
have walked by the flesh and therefore sinned by
_____ *(act).*
Thank You for cleansing me of all unrighteousness. I
ask that You would enable me to walk by the Spirit
and not carry out the desires of the flesh. In Jesus'
name, I pray. Amen.

It is our responsibility not to allow sin to reign in our
mortal bodies by not using our bodies as instruments of
unrighteousness (Romans 6:12, 13). If you are struggling
or have struggled with sexual sins (pornography,
masturbation, sexual promiscuity, etc) or are
experiencing sexual difficulty in your marriage, pray as
follows:

Lord,
I ask You to reveal to my mind every sexual use of my
body as an instrument of unrighteousness. In Jesus'
precious name, I pray. Amen.

As the Lord brings to your mind every sexual misuse of
your body, whether it was done to you – rape, incest or
other sexual abuse – or willingly by you, renounce every
occasion:

Lord,
I renounce _____ (misuse of your body) with
_____ (person) and ask You to
break that bond.

Now commit your body to the Lord by praying:

Lord,
I renounce all these uses of my body as an instrument
of unrighteousness and by so doing ask You to break all

bondages Satan has brought into my life through that involvement. I confess my participation. I now present my body to You as a living sacrifice, holy and acceptable to You and I reserve the sexual use of my body only for marriage. I renounce the lie of Satan that my body is not clean, that it is dirty or in any way unacceptable as a result of my past sexual experiences. Lord, I thank You that You have totally cleansed and forgiven me, that You love and accept me unconditionally. Therefore, I can accept myself. And I choose to do so, to accept myself and my body as cleansed. In Jesus' name, Amen.

Special prayers for specific problems

Homosexuality

Lord,
I renounce the lie that You have created me or anyone
else to be homosexual, and I affirm that You clearly
forbid homosexual behaviour. I accept myself as a child
of God and declare that You created me a
(man/woman). I renounce any bondages of Satan that
have perverted my relationship with others. I announce
that I am free to relate to the opposite sex in the way
that You intended. In Jesus' name, Amen.

Abortion

Lord,
I confess that I did not assume stewardship of the life
You entrusted to me. I choose to accept Your
forgiveness, and I now commit that child to You for
Your care in eternity. In Jesus' name, Amen.

Suicidal Tendencies

Lord,
I renounce suicidal thoughts and any attempts I have
made to take my own life or in any way injure myself. I
renounce the lie that life is hopeless and that I can find
peace and freedom by taking my own life. Satan is a
thief and he comes to steal, kill and destroy. I choose to
be a good steward of the physical life that You have
entrusted to me. In Jesus' name, I pray. Amen.

Eating disorders or self-mutilation

Lord,
I renounce the lie that my value as a person is
dependent upon my physical beauty, my weight or size.
I renounce cutting myself, vomiting, using laxatives or
starving myself as a means of cleansing myself of evil
or altering my appearance. I announce that only the
blood of the Lord Jesus Christ cleanses me from sin. I
accept the reality that there may be sin present in me
because of the lies I have believed and the wrongful use
of my body, but I renounce the lie that I am evil or that
any part of my body is evil. My body is the temple of
the Holy Spirit and I belong to You, Lord. I receive Your
love and acceptance of me. In Jesus' name, Amen.

Substance abuse

Lord,
I confess that I have misused substances (alcohol,
tobacco, food, prescription or street drugs) for the
purpose of pleasure, to escape reality or to cope with
difficult situations – resulting in the abuse of my body,
the harmful programming of my mind and the
quenching of the Holy Spirit. I ask Your forgiveness. I
renounce any satanic connection or influence in my life
through my misuse of chemicals or food. I cast my
anxiety onto Christ Who loves me, and I commit
myself to yield no longer to substance abuse, but to the
Holy Spirit. I ask You, Heavenly Father, to fill me with
Your Holy Spirit. In Jesus' name, Amen.

Drivenness and perfectionism

Lord,
I renounce the lie that my self-worth is dependent upon
my ability to perform. I announce the truth that my
identity and sense of worth are found in who I am as
Your child. I renounce seeking the approval and
acceptance of other people, and I choose to believe that
I am already approved and accepted in Christ because
of His death and resurrection for me. I choose to believe
the truth that I have been saved, not by deeds done in
righteousness, but according to Your mercy. I choose to
believe that I am no longer under the curse of the law,
because Christ became a curse for me. I receive the free
gift of life in Christ and choose to abide in Him. I
renounce striving for perfection by living under the law.
By Your grace, Heavenly Father, I choose from this day
forward to walk by faith according to what You have
said is true by the power of Your Holy Spirit. In Jesus'
name, Amen.

Plaguing fears

A fuller treatment of plaguing fears can be found in
Appendix 2. You might find this helpful if you have
been prone to many fears.

Dear Heavenly Father,
I acknowledge You as the only legitimate fear object in
my life. You are the only ever-present and all-knowing
God and the only means by which all other fears can
be expelled. You are my sanctuary. You have not given
me a spirit of timidity, but of power and love and
self-control. I confess that I have allowed the fear of
man and the fear of death to exercise control over my
life instead of trusting You. I now renounce all other

fear objects and worship You only. I pray that You would fill me with Your Holy Spirit that I may live my life and speak Your Word with boldness. In Jesus' name, I pray. Amen.

Prejudice and bigotry

Dear Heavenly Father,
I know that You love everyone equally and that You do not show favouritism, but You accept people from every nation who fear You and do what is right (Acts 10:34). You do not judge people based on race, gender, culture, economic or social status (Galatians 3:28). I confess that I have too often prejudged others or regarded myself as superior because of these things. I have not always been a minister of reconciliation, but have been a proud agent of division through my attitudes, words and deeds. I repent of all hateful bigotry and proud prejudice and I ask You, Lord, to reveal to my mind all the specific ways in which this form of pride has corrupted my heart and mind. I confess and renounce the prideful sin of prejudice against _____ (group). I thank You for Your forgiveness, Lord, and ask You to change my heart and make me a loving agent of reconciliation with (group). In Jesus' name, Amen.

After you have confessed all known sin, end this step by praying:

Dear Heavenly Father,
I now confess these sins to You and claim forgiveness and cleansing through the blood of the Lord Jesus Christ. I cancel all ground that evil spirits have gained through my wilful involvement in sin. I ask this in the wonderful name of my Lord and Saviour, Jesus Christ. Amen.

Step 7

Acquiescence vs. Renunciation

Acquiescence is passively giving in or agreeing without consent. The last step to freedom is to renounce the sins of your ancestors and any curses which may have been placed on you. In giving the Ten Commandments, God said: 'You shall not make for yourself an idol, or any likeness of what is in heaven above or on the earth beneath or in the water under the earth. You shall not worship them or serve them; for I, the LORD your God, am a jealous God, visiting the iniquity of the fathers on the children, on the third and fourth generations of those who hate Me' (Exodus 20:4, 5).

Familiar spirits can be passed on from one generation to the next if not renounced and if your new spiritual heritage in Christ is not proclaimed. You are not guilty for the sin of any ancestor, but, because of their sin, Satan may have gained access to your family. This is not to deny that many problems are transmitted genetically or acquired from an immoral atmosphere. All three conditions can predispose an individual to a particular sin. In addition, deceived people may try to curse you, or satanic groups may try to target you. You have all the authority and protection you need in Christ to stand against such curses and assignments.

Ask the Lord to reveal to your mind the sins and

iniquities of your ancestors by praying the following prayer:

Dear Heavenly Father,
I thank You that I am a new creation in Christ. I desire
to obey Your command to honour my mother and
father, but I also acknowledge that my physical
heritage has not been perfect. I ask You to reveal to my
mind the sins and iniquities of my ancestors in order to
confess, renounce and forsake them. In Jesus' name, I
pray. Amen.

Now claim your position and protection in Christ by making the following declaration verbally, and then by humbling yourself before God in prayer.

Declaration

I here and now reject and disown all the sins and
iniquities of my ancestors, including _____ (name/s).
As one who has been delivered from the power of
darkness and translated into the kingdom of God's
dear Son, I cancel out all demonic working that has
been passed on to me from my ancestors. As one who
has been crucified and raised with Jesus Christ and
who sits with Him in heavenly places, I renounce all
satanic assignments that are directed toward me and
my ministry, and I cancel every curse that Satan and
his workers have put on me. I announce to Satan and
all his forces that Christ became a curse for me
(Galatians 3:13) when He died for my sins on the cross.
I reject any and every way in which Satan may claim
ownership of me. I belong to the Lord Jesus Christ who
purchased me with His own blood. I reject all other
blood sacrifices whereby Satan may claim ownership of

me. I declare myself to be eternally and completely signed over and committed to the Lord Jesus Christ. By the authority I have in Jesus Christ, I now command every spiritual enemy of the Lord Jesus Christ to leave my presence. I commit myself to my heavenly Father to do His will from this day forward.

Prayer

Dear Heavenly Father,
I come to You as Your child purchased by the blood of the Lord Jesus Christ. You are the Lord of the universe and the Lord of my life. I submit my body to You as an instrument of righteousness, a living sacrifice, that I may glorify You in my body. I now ask You to fill me with Your Holy Spirit. I commit myself to the renewing of my mind in order to prove that Your will is good, perfect and acceptable for me. All this I do in the name and authority of the Lord Jesus Christ. Amen.

Aftercare

Once you have secured your freedom by going through these seven steps, you may find demonic influences attempting to come back in, days or even months later. One person shared that she heard a spirit say to her mind, 'I'm back,' two days after she had been set free. 'No, you're not!' she proclaimed aloud. The attack ceased immediately. One victory does not constitute winning the war. Freedom must be maintained. After completing these steps, one jubilant lady asked, 'Will I always be like this?' I told her that she would stay free as long as she remained in right relationship with God. 'Even if you slip and fall,' I encouraged, 'you know how to get right with God again.'

One victim of incredible atrocities shared this illustration: 'It's like being forced to play a game with an ugly stranger in my own home. I kept losing and wanted to quit, but the ugly stranger wouldn't let me. Finally I called the police [a higher authority], and they came and escorted the stranger out. He knocked on the door trying to regain entry, but this time I recognised his voice and didn't let him in.'

What a beautiful illustration of gaining freedom in Christ. We call upon Jesus, the ultimate authority, and He escorts the enemy out of our lives. Know the truth, stand firm and resist the evil one. Seek out good Christian fellowship, and commit yourself to regular times of Bible study and prayer. God loves you and will never leave or forsake you.

Freedom must be maintained. You have won a very

important battle in an ongoing war. Freedom is yours as long as you keep choosing the truth and standing firm in the strength of the Lord. If new memories should surface or if you become aware of lies that you have believed or other non-Christian experiences you have had, renounce them and choose the truth. Some have found it helpful to go through the steps again. As you do, read the instructions carefully.

For your encouragement and further study, read *Victory Over the Darkness* (or the youth version *Stomping Out the Darkness*), *The Bondage Breaker* (adult or youth version) and *Living Free*. If you are a parent, read *Spiritual Protection for Your Children*. Also, to maintain your freedom, we suggest the following:

1. Be involved in a loving, caring church fellowship where you can be open and honest with others.

2. Read your Bible every day. Memorise key verses.

3. Learn to take every thought captive to the obedience of Christ. Assume responsibility for your thought life, reject the lie, choose the truth and stand firm in your true identity as a child of God in Christ.

4. Don't drift away! It is very easy to get lazy in your thoughts and revert back to old habits or patterns of thinking. Share your struggles openly with a trusted friend. You need at least one friend who will stand with you.

5. Don't expect other people to fight your battles for you. Others can help, but they can't think, pray, read the Bible or choose the truth for you.

6. Continue to seek your identity and sense of worth in Christ. Read *Living Free* and the devotional, *Daily in*

Christ. Renew your mind with the truth that your acceptance, security and significance are in Christ by saturating your mind with the following truths. Read the entire list of who you are 'In Christ' (page 54 below) and the Doctrinal Affirmation (page 25 above) aloud every morning and evening over the next several weeks (and look up the verses).

7. Commit yourself to daily prayer. You can pray these suggested prayers often and with confidence. Let the words come from your heart as well as your lips.

Daily prayer

Dear Heavenly Father,
I honour You as my sovereign Lord. I acknowledge that You are always present with me. You are the only all-powerful and wise God. You are kind and loving in all Your ways. I love You and thank You that I am united with Christ and spiritually alive in Him. I choose not to love the world, and I crucify the flesh and all its passions.

I thank You for the life that I now have in Christ, and I ask You to fill me with Your Holy Spirit, that I may live my life free from sin. I declare my dependence upon You, and I take my stand against Satan and all his lying ways. I choose to believe the truth and I refuse to be discouraged. You are the God of all hope, and I am confident that You will meet my needs as I seek to live according to Your Word. I express with confidence that I can live a responsible life through Christ who strengthens me.

I now take my stand against Satan and command him and all his evil spirits to depart from me. I put on the whole armour of God. I submit my body as a living sacrifice and renew my mind by the living Word of God in order that I may prove that the will of God is good, acceptable and perfect. I pray these things in the precious name of my Lord and Saviour, Jesus Christ. Amen.

Bedtime prayer

Thank You, Lord, that You have brought me into Your family and have blessed me with every spiritual blessing in the heavenly realms in Christ. Thank You for providing this time of renewal through sleep. I accept it as part of Your perfect plan for Your children, and I trust You to guard my mind and my body during my sleep. As I have meditated on You and Your truth during this day, I choose to let these thoughts continue in my mind while I am asleep. I commit myself to You for Your protection from every attempt of Satan or his demons to attack me during sleep. I commit myself to You as my Rock, my Fortress and Resting Place. I pray in the strong name of the Lord Jesus Christ. Amen.

Cleansing the home

After removing all articles of false worship from your home, pray aloud in every room if necessary:

Heavenly Father,
We/I acknowledge that You are the Lord of heaven and earth. In Your sovereign power and love, You have given us/me all things richly to enjoy. Thank You for this place to live. We/I claim this home for our/my family as a place of spiritual safety and protection from all the

attacks of the enemy. As children/a child of God seated with Christ in the heavenly realm, we/I command every evil spirit claiming ground in the structures and furnishings of this place, based on the activities of previous occupants, to leave and never return. We/I renounce all curses and spells utilised against this place. We/I ask You, Heavenly Father, to post guardian angels around this home/room to guard it from attempts of the enemy to enter and disturb Your purpose for us/me. We/I thank You, Lord, for doing this, and pray in the name of the Lord Jesus Christ. Amen.

Living in a non-Christian environment

After removing all articles of false worship from your room, pray aloud in the space allotted to you:

Thank You, Heavenly Father, for my place to live and be renewed by sleep. I ask You to set aside my room as a place of spiritual safety for me. I renounce any allegiance given to false gods or spirits by other occupants, and I renounce any claim to this room by Satan based on activities of past occupants or me. On the basis of my position as a child of God and a joint-heir with Christ who has all authority in heaven and on earth, I command all evil spirits to leave this place and never return. I ask You, Heavenly Father, to appoint guardian angels to protect me while I live here. I pray this in the name of the Lord Jesus Christ. Amen.

In Christ ...
I am accepted

John 1:12	I am God's child.
John 15:15	I am Christ's friend.
Romans 5:1	I have been justified.
1 Corinthians 6:17	I am united with the Lord, and I am one spirit with Him.
1 Corinthians 6:20	I have been bought with a price. I belong to God.
1 Corinthians 12:27	I am a member of Christ's Body.
Ephesians 1:1	I am a saint.
Ephesians 1:5	I have been adopted as God's child.
Ephesians 2:18	I have direct access to God through the Holy Spirit.
Colossians 1:14	I have been redeemed and forgiven of all my sins.
Colossians 2:10	I am complete in Christ.

In Christ ...
I am secure

Romans 8:1, 2	I am free from condemnation.
Romans 8:28	I am assured that all things work together for good.
Romans 8:31–34	I am free from any condemning charges against me.
Romans 8:35–39	I cannot be separated from the love of God.
2 Corinthians 1:21, 22	I have been established, anointed and sealed by God.
Colossians 3:3	I am hidden with Christ in God.
Philippians 1:6	I am confident that the good work God has begun in me will be perfected.
Philippians 3:20	I am a citizen of heaven.
2 Timothy 1:7	I have not been given a spirit of fear, but of power, love and a sound mind.
Hebrews 4:16	I can find grace and mercy to help in time of need.
1 John 5:18	I am born of God and the evil one cannot touch me.

In Christ ...
I am significant

Matthew 5:13, 14	I am the salt and light of the earth.
John 15:1, 5	I am a branch of the true Vine, a channel of His life.
John 15:16	I have been chosen and appointed to bear fruit.
Acts 1:8	I am a personal witness of Christ.
1 Corinthians 3:16	I am God's temple.
2 Corinthians 5:17–21	I am a minister of reconciliation for God.
2 Corinthians 6:1	I am God's fellow-worker (1 Corinthians 3:9).
Ephesians 2:6	I am seated with Christ in the heavenly realm.
Ephesians 2:10	I am God's workmanship.
Ephesians 3:12	I may approach God with freedom and confidence.
Philippians 4:13	I can do all things through Christ Who strengthens me.

How To Establish A Freedom Ministry in Your Church

Afterword for church leaders by Steve Goss, Director, Freedom In Christ Ministries (UK)

Although *Steps To Freedom In Christ* can be used by individuals on their own, it is usually preferable for Christians to claim their freedom in the context of a supportive church environment.

Shinfield Baptist Church near Reading was one of the first churches in the UK to establish its own freedom ministry based on the teaching in *Victory Over the Darkness* and *The Bondage Breaker* together with *Steps To Freedom In Christ*.

According to the Pastor, Rev. Ian Greig, 'It's been the key to so many pastoral problems that we couldn't unlock by conventional means. We taught the principles in a group context first and then gave people the opportunity to go through "Steps To Freedom" individually.'

About half of the church has now been through *Steps To Freedom In Christ* helped by one or two others in a simple, non-threatening process that typically takes just one evening. In every case, there has been a real spiritual release and growth. In some cases people would describe their experience as a complete turnaround.

Sara Hudson, Deacon, says, 'I had got past the point of believing that any new ministry could have a genuinely dramatic effect, but the Steps To Freedom course has done this for me and others. And actually, it's not some new-fangled theory – it's just biblical truth applied in a very good and helpful framework.'

According to Ian Greig, 'So many people struggle to try to become the way Jesus wants us to be. This methodology makes understanding who we are in Christ and taking hold of the freedom that is ours in Christ really accessible to all. It's difficult to imagine any church that would not really be released by using the principles developed by Dr Anderson.'

There is nothing 'new' in Freedom In Christ teaching – to quote the deacon above again, it is 'just biblical truth'. But it's applied in such a way that it's not difficult to establish an effective ongoing ministry that has the added bonus of being exceptionally kind to those taking part.

Training a capable team of lay people to help people through the steps is within the reach of even the smallest fellowship. The concepts are designed for non-specialists and are completely transferable. There are many resources to help, from tapes to videos to ready-made training courses.

Many churches use *Breaking Through To Spiritual Maturity*, a 13-week group study of *Victory Over the Darkness* and *The Bondage Breaker*, to get started. It makes an ideal follow-up to an Alpha course and prepares people very well for their own freedom appointment (during which they go through *Steps To Freedom In Christ*).

Once some of your people have been through the steps, others will notice the difference and the whole thing will start to snowball. You could end up with a radically different church – many have!

To take this further, the first thing to do is to familiarise yourself with the key concepts by reading *Victory Over the Darkness* and *The Bondage Breaker*. Then get in touch with Freedom In Christ UK for an up-to-date list of resources, conferences and training programmes.

When you are ready to start you will also want to take advantage of the UK Freedom Fellowship, a network of like-minded Christians and churches who are ministering to their community using *Steps To Freedom In Christ*. Members receive regular news, helpful information and encouragement. Contact Freedom In Christ UK for further details.

Freedom In Christ UK

Freedom In Christ Ministries (UK), PO Box 2842, Reading RG2 9RT.

E-mail: ukoffice@ficm.org

The main Freedom In Christ website contains a whole host of helpful information. Find it at ficm.org.

Appendix 1: **God's Love**

I renounce the lie that my Father God is ...	I joyfully accept the truth that my Father God is ...
distant and disinterested	intimate and involved (Psalm139:1–18)
insensitive and uncaring	kind and compassionate (Psalm 103:8–14)
stern and demanding	accepting and filled with joy and love (Romans 15:7; Zephaniah 3:17)
passive and cold	warm and affectionate (Isaiah 40:11; Hosea 11:3–4)
absent or too busy for me	always with me and eager to be with me (Hebrews 13:5; Jeremiah 31:20; Ezekiel 34:11–16)
never satisfied with what I do, impatient or angry	patient and slow to anger (Exodus 34:6; 2 Peter 3:9)
mean, cruel or abusive	loving, gentle and protective of me (Jeremiah 31:3; Isaiah 42:3; Psalm 18:2)
trying to take all the fun out of life	trustworthy and wants to give me a full life; His will is good, perfect and acceptable for me (Lamentations 3:22–23; John 10:10; Romans 12:1–2)
controlling or manipulative	full of grace and mercy, and He gives me freedom to fail (Hebrews 4:15–16; Luke 15:11–16)
condemning or unforgiving	tender-hearted and forgiving; His heart and arms are always open to me (Psalm 130:1–4; Luke 15:17–24)
nit-picking, exacting or perfectionistic	committed to my growth and proud of me as His growing child (Romans 8:28–29; Hebrews 12:5–11; 2 Corinthians 7:14)
I am the apple of His eye! Deuteronomy 32:9–10	

Appendix 2: Plaguing Fears

Dear Heavenly Father,
I confess to You that I have listened to the devil's roar
and have allowed fear to master me. I have not always
walked by faith in You but instead have focused on my
feelings and circumstances (2 Corinthians 4:16–18;
5:7). Thank You for forgiving me for my unbelief. Right
now I renounce the spirit of fear and affirm the truth
that You have not given me a spirit of fear but of
power, love and a sound mind (2 Timothy 1:7). Lord,
please reveal to my mind now all the fears that have
been controlling me so I can renounce them and be free
to walk by faith in You.

I thank You for the freedom You give me to walk by
faith and not by fear. In Jesus' powerful name, I pray.
Amen.

The following list may help you recognise some of the
fears the devil has used to keep you from walking by
faith. Tick the ones that apply to your life. Write down
any others that the Spirit of God brings to your mind.

Then, one by one, renounce those fears out loud, using
the suggested renunciation below.

❏ Fear of death

❏ Fear of Satan

❏ Fear of failure

❏ Fear of rejection by people

❏ Fear of disapproval

❏ Fear of not being loved by God

❏ Fear of never loving or being loved by others

❏ Fear of embarrassment

❏ Fear of being victimised by crime

- ❏ Fear of becoming/being homosexual
- ❏ Fear of financial problems
- ❏ Fear of never getting married
- ❏ Fear of the death of a loved one
- ❏ Fear of being a hopeless case
- ❏ Fear of losing salvation
- ❏ Fear of having committed the unpardonable sin

- ❏ Fear of marriage
- ❏ Fear of divorce
- ❏ Fear of going crazy
- ❏ Fear of pain/illness
- ❏ Fear of the future
- ❏ Fear of confrontation
- ❏ Fear of specific individuals (list)
- ❏ Other specific fears that come to mind now

I renounce the fear of _____
because God has not given me a spirit of fear (2 Timothy 1:7). I choose to live by faith in God Who has promised to protect me and meet all my needs as I walk by faith in Him (Psalm 27:1; Matthew 6:33, 34).

After you have finished renouncing all the specific fears you have allowed to control you, pray the following prayer.

Dear Heavenly Father,
I thank You that You are trustworthy. I choose to believe You, even when my feelings and circumstances tell me to fear. You have told me not to fear, for You are with me; not to look about me anxiously, for You are my God. You will strengthen me, help me and surely uphold me with Your righteous right hand (Isaiah 41:10). I pray this with faith in the name of Jesus my Master. Amen.

Freedom In Christ In The UK

Church Leaders - can we help you?

Thousands of churches around the world use Neil Anderson's material to help Christians find their freedom in Christ. If you are a church leader and would like to establish your own freedom ministry, Freedom In Christ Ministries (UK) is here to help. We run a programme of conferences and training. And we are always more than happy to offer free advice.

Send for our Resource Catalogue

Send for our full colour catalogue of Neil Anderson books, videos and audiocassettes. It includes resources for individuals, for churches, and for local freedom ministries as well as for specialist freedom areas such as fear, depression and addiction. It's also crammed with hints and tips.

Join the UK Freedom Fellowship

If you are ministering to your community using Neil Anderson's materials, join our network of like-minded Christians and receive regular news, encouragement and affirmation. Open to anyone involved in a local freedom ministry or considering setting one up.

For details of any of the above write to us at:

Freedom In Christ Ministries (UK), PO Box 2842, READING RG2 9RT

Or e-mail us: ukoffice@ficm.org

You can find the Freedom In Christ worldwide web site at www.ficm.org

"It is for FREEDOM that Christ has set us FREE"
Galatians 5:1

Freedom in Christ is an international, interdenominational ministry which exists to glorify God by prayer-fully and strategically equipping and resourcing churches, Christian organisations, and mission groups in keeping with the Great Commandment in order to accomplish the Great Commission.

Please note that Freedom In Christ Ministries (UK) does not arrange personal freedom appointments or offer personal advice but works by equipping local churches to do this.